EXTREME SPORTS

Written and photographed by David Spurdens

TOP THAT! Kids™

Copyright © 2004 Top That! Publishing plc,
Top That! Publishing, 27023 McBean Parkway, #408 Valencia, CA 91355
Top That! is a Registered Trademark of Top That! Publishing plc
All rights reserved
www.topthatpublishing.com

Contents

Introduction	3
History	4
Skateboarding	6
Surfing	9
Kite Surfing	14
Sandboarding	16
Snowboarding	18
Ice and Rock Climbing	22
Polar Trekking	23
Sand Yachting	24
Hang-gliding and Paragliding	26
Skiing Off-Piste	29
Downhill Skiing	31
Kayaking	32
BMX	34
Mountain Biking	36
Bungee Jumping	40
Cliff Jumping	41
BASE Jumping	42
Motorsports	45
Final Word	48

Introduction

From kite surfing to paragliding, this book takes you on a white-knuckle ride into the dangerous world of extreme sports.

Dangerous
Extreme sports are cool and exciting—they are also very dangerous! So before we start our trip through the world of extreme sport, a quick word of warning. All of the sports shown in this book have been undertaken by trained professionals after years of training.

NEVER try to copy any of the tricks shown in this book!

Best of the Best
All the people contained in this book I have personally met and photographed; each one has spent years fine-tuning their individual skills to be the best in the world, whether on the big waves of Hawaii or snowboarding in the Alps. To be the best, they have worked tirelessly, endlessly traveling to do the sports they love. Whether their sport

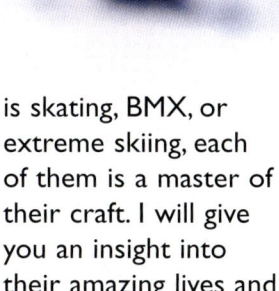

is skating, BMX, or extreme skiing, each of them is a master of their craft. I will give you an insight into their amazing lives and the stories behind them. Be safe!

*David Spurdens,
Extreme Sports
Photographer.*

History

From gladiatorial combat and glacier hiking to surfing and snowboarding, extreme sports have always played an integral part in our culture.

Jousting
In medieval times, knights in England practiced a sport called jousting. The sport involved two horsemen galloping at speed toward each other with a long jousting pole and attempting to knock each other off their horse—that's extreme!

Glacier Hiking
In recent years an ancient European was found frozen in a glacier in Austria. Evidence suggests that he fell down a crevasse while crossing a glacier. Today, glacier trekking is considered so extreme that nobody would attempt it on their own.

Basic Bungee
The forerunner to bungee jumping was witnessed on Pentecost Island, South Pacific, hundreds of years ago. As a test of manhood, men tied vines to their feet and launched from a platform in the same way bungee jumpers do today.

Nat Young, 55, from Australia, rides the biggest wave of the Quiksilver Masters in Hawaii 2003.

History

Hawaiian Kings
Started by Hawaiian fishermen hundreds of years ago, surfing is one of the oldest forms of extreme sport. It is now a worldwide sporting phenomenon.

Skiing off a 50 ft cliff.

Extreme Technology
Most of the sports featured in this book have been invented in the last century, as they rely on designs and materials technology that has only been available in recent times. From complex parachuting materials to plastics used for boarding, we owe a lot to the inventors who made these sports possible.

BASE jumping in the Gorge du Verdon, France.

Extreme Fun
In the past, people did things that we class today as extreme sports in order to survive—from collecting food and traveling from a to b, to proving their worth in society. Today, we do extreme sports for one reason only—fun! This book proves extreme sports enthusiasts equate fun with adrenaline!

Horse racing on a frozen lake in St. Moritz, Switzerland.

Skateboarding

England's Mark Munson describes what it is like to fly high above the "table top" in French ski resort, Bourg St. Maurice—on a skateboard!

King of Cool

"I was in the Alps snowboarding when a friend spotted the ski jumps on the other side of the lake. We went to check them out and I immediately thought how cool it would be to ride the killer jump on my skateboard.

Ice Cold

At first I thought about a lip trick on the ramp, then I thought it would be better to air off into the lake. As the lake is frozen for most of the year I knew the water would be ice cold. Some friends said that if they jumped in first I had to do it!

Friendly Advice

Reassured that my friends on the trip would get cold as well, I decided to go for it. I had wanted to try rodeo flips for a while, but when I realized just how high the ramp was I ditched my board and focused on not killing myself!

Skateboarding

Skateboarding off a ski ramp on a lake in France.

A vert ramp in Cornwall.

Landing
I landed in the lake and it was colder than I had expected. As I swam for the side my arms and legs started locking up because of the cold—it took over an hour for me to stop shaking. I would love to do it again, but next time with a wetsuit!"

REMEMBER—
NEVER, EVER TRY
THIS YOURSELF!

Skateboarding

Big Business
Skateboarding is big business today. The top stars are now able to focus on improving their skills by gaining lucrative sponsorship deals with clothing and sports equipment manufacturers. This photo was taken in the Bourg St. Maurice Skate Park, France for a shoe advertisement.

Surfing

Surfing is a difficult and exhilarating sport. The following pages show you how the pros tackle the toughest breaks on the planet.

Way of Life
Surfing your first clean-breaking wave is an amazing feeling. In fact, many people who take up surfing are quickly addicted and change their entire lifestyle to improve their surfing prowess. Great surfers follow the best waves around the world, but the rest of us can find excellent breaks closer to home without too much difficulty.

Even professional surfers wipe out in big waves.

Perfect Wave
About 70% of Earth is covered in water, so it stands to reason that, at any time, there will be great waves waiting to be surfed. From big wave surfing in Hawaii to renowned swells on the coasts of Europe, as long as you can get to the beach, you will find great waves!

The Pipeline
One of the world's most famous surf spots is the Pipeline, situated on the north shore of Oahu, Hawaii. The wipeout, below, was taken at the "2002 Pipeline Masters" competition.

Surfing

It is difficult not to be excited by the sheer force and magnitude of big waves and the way in which pro surfers make them look easy!

Six World Champions
1. Six of the world's greatest surfers line up in Hawaii, including Shaun Thompson, Mark Richards, Martin Potter, "Rabbit" Bartholomew and Tom Curren.

Crowd Pleaser
2. Showing perfect poise, this surfer demonstrates how to pull off a crowd-pleasing carve at a round of the surfing world championships. Carving through warm, deep-blue seas is the ultimate thrill for most surfers.

Riding the Face!
3. Speeding ahead of the breaking face, this surfer expresses his joy by trailing his hand in the face of the wave. This is truly surfing at its best!

Surfing

Longboards
4. Descended from the Malibu board, the ultra-stable, but hard-to-maneuver, longboard is great for impressive tricks such as the "hang ten" and "sunrise."

UK Surf Style
5. You don't necessarily have to be in the USA or Australia to catch great waves. This shot was taken in Cornwall, UK.

Crowded Surf Spot
6. Unless you are a pro and among friends, dropping in on other surfers' waves is really not a good idea!

Surfing

Huge Faces
1. Huge faces like the one pictured above are common at Hawaii's Pipeline break.

Backdoor in Hawaii
2. Not quite as famous as the Pipeline, the "Backdoor" in Hawaii is a formidable break and offers some excellent surf.

Body Boarding
3. Body boards are an excellent way to get into surfing. Cheap to buy, you catch waves in a flat position and use the side edges to steer the board, as pictured.

Surfing

Big Wave Weather
Big waves are most common when there is a depression in the ocean and also high pressure on the coastline.

Swell
As a result of the depression, a swell builds in the ocean, arriving at the coast within a couple of days, causing huge waves.

Shell Waves
Reefs and rock shelves, such as those at Waimea Bay, Hawaii (below), impede the progress of the water, causing it to rise up into a massive wave.

Big waves, like the one pictured below, have immense power. Novice surfers should not venture into the sea in such conditions.

13

Kite Surfing

Ripping the faces of huge waves, insane jumps, tricks, transitions, wipeouts, and superhuman endurance—this is kite surfing!

Kite Skiing at the North Pole
1. A kite skier journeying 800 miles north of the Arctic Circle in −67°F temperatures.

Learning to Kite Surf
2. Picking up the basics of kite surfing is easy if you have board skills; you just need to learn how to control the kite. Kite surfing clubs and societies operate around the world to help you get into this great extreme sport.

Kite Surfing

Beautiful Brighton
Jason Verness boosts an air at Brighton Pier, England: "Wave ahead! Power up and touch 35–40 mph before hitting the water on the face of the wave rearing up from the ocean. I whip the kite back above me and go into orbit! Timing is perfect, and my flexifoil kite's pulling me higher as it catches the gust. I begin to count airtime —5 seconds, 6, 7— then the water's coming back up and I make a perfect touchdown to surf away on the next wave."

Sandboarding

Mark Hayman has spent seven years as a pro snowboarder. This is his first-hand account of tackling the Dune du Pyla, France, on a sandboard.

Dune du Pyla

"Nicki Watts and I are at the 350 ft. Dune du Pyla—the biggest in Europe—and, we've hatched a plan to go sandboarding. Lots of tourists are staring incredulously as we strap snowboards to our feet and prepare to set off in the blazing sun.

Nicki Watts carving up the sand.

Sticky Moments

Once I'm moving, the old instincts take over—plenty of speed, keep the body open, and go for it! Sand is weird; sticky to about 15 mph then, suddenly, very fast and unforgiving if you get the balance even a little wrong.

Thirsty Work

The only problem, I contemplate later that evening, is that they really do need to install a draglift. Walking up the 350 ft. dune is very thirsty work!"

Perfect balance is essential for sandboarding.

Sandboarding

Mark Hayman calmly leads the way down Europe's biggest sand dune.

Snowboarding

Snowboarding was pioneered by Jake Burton and Tom Simms in America. Since then, it has taken the world by storm.

Snowboarding requires stamina and speed.

Getting Started
Snowboarding requires stamina, speed, strength, and excellent balance. So before you hit the powder, it is a good idea to work on your basic fitness.

Fitness
Cardiovascular exercises such as running and aerobics are good ways to build up basic fitness. As with any sport, specific muscles are used in snowboarding. Ask your local gym instructor for advice on exercises to build up your legs and lower back.

Warming Up
Warming up is very important for snowboarders as you will spend a lot of time sitting on lifts waiting to get to the top of your chosen slope.

Yoga
Yoga is an excellent form of exercise for snowboarders, skateboarders, and surfers as it helps to build strength and increases flexibility.

A mid-air grab.

Simple Exercises
Spread your legs and bend down as far as you can, keeping your legs straight. Now do the same with your legs together. These exercises will stretch your back, leg, and shoulder muscles.

Turning on a ridge can create amazing powder sprays.

Snowboarding

Goofy or Natural?

In most sports, people have a preference for the right or left side. In snowboarding this is described as being "goofy" or "natural." Goofy boarders place their right foot forward, while natural boarders have their left foot forward.

Getting some big air in the Alps.

A "Tindy"—an illegal grab!

Test

Lay the snowboard on flat snow. Place your right foot just behind the front binding and push off as if you are riding a scooter. Now try this technique with your other foot. Whichever feels the most comfortable determines whether you are goofy or natural.

Don't try this at home!

Snowboarding

Dry Ski Slopes
If you don't live near a snow-covered mountain range, or if it's summer, then a local dry slope is a great place to find your snowboarding feet. Most dry ski slopes hire out equipment, so you needn't break the bank in order to find out if snowboarding is the sport for you!

Off-piste snowboarding.

Big jumps separate the men from the boys.

Accident Prevention
Put a pillow down the back of your pants and tape your fingers up so they don't get caught in the dendex. This is the sensible way to practice before hitting the slopes.

The Next Step
Once you have become fairly proficient at snowboarding, the whole mountain opens up. However, unless you're an expert you must always take a guide with you if you venture off-piste.

On-Piste
On-piste you can carve down the slopes and hit the snowpark to try to learn some of the tricks that your heroes perform. With proper instruction and safety gear, the halfpipe is lots of fun!

A boarder trailing his hand in the powder surf-style!

Snowboarding

Off-Piste
Off-piste and big mountain riding, as featured in this book, can be very dangerous. Remember—ALWAYS get a guide that knows the area, then those big powder turns are yours for the taking!

Ice and Rock Climbing

"Nothing beats the feeling that you get when you reach the top of a climb."—Mark Hayman.

Mind over Matter

"You know that you shouldn't be hanging onto a frozen waterfall by two tiny axe blades and crampons, or clinging to a sheer cliff hundreds of feet up, but you can't stop smiling when you realize that's exactly what you are doing.

Mark Hayman climbing a frozen waterfall.

Ice Climbing

As with most extreme sports, this one really is dangerous. You have to be perfect in your reading of the terrain, your choice of equipment and route, and your technical know-how and fitness. You get out of ice climbing very much what you put in. Make a mistake and it will be bad. But boy, that feeling when you reach the top! Sometimes, such as when climbing a 300 ft. frozen waterfall, the only thing that keeps you going is the will to succeed."

Mark Hayman clinging to a 300 ft sheer cliff face.

Polar Trekking

Frostbite, hungry polar bears and fatigue—polar trekking is no walk in the park!

Walk of Your Life

If your idea of a good walk involves plodding a block or two and back, then ice trekking is not for you! In these amazing pictures, British Royal Marines Shaun Chapple and Alan Chambers are training hard for a trek to the North Pole. They are walking on a frozen sea 800 miles north of the Arctic Circle. The following year they made it to the Pole.

Trekking 800 miles north of the Arctic Circle.

Extreme Conditions

Here Shaun and Alan are hauling their sleds across ice rubble in temperatures of $-67°$ F! As well as having to cope with the temperatures, the ice can break up and cause them to fall into the freezing Arctic waters. Polar bears searching for the next meal are another BIG threat!

Training for an expedition to the North Pole.

Sand Yachting

Traveling in a buggy, sometimes on one wheel, at 50 mph with the ground just inches below makes sand yachting a far cry from a rowboat!

Pioneer
Sand yachting was first thought of by Prince Maurice of Nassau in the 16th century. He thought that creating a sail car powered by the sea breezes would surely produce impressive speed across the sand—he was right! It was another 300 years before the idea was resurrected, when brothers André and Benjamin Dumont designed the first vehicles to be used in competition in France in 1898.

21st Century
Today, the sport is still going strong, and sand or land yachting can provide an extreme buzz. You sit in a plastic frame with a sail above, and powered by the wind, you can reach speeds of 50 mph.

Wheelies
At these speeds the sand yacht is frequently up from its usual three wheels to sometimes two, and occasionally one! There are no brakes, so your direction is all-important.

Eco-Friendly
It's an environmentally-friendly sport, like most extreme sports, powered solely by the wind with no exhaust fumes. This fact is one of the reasons that it seems to be becoming increasingly popular.

A sand yachter races to reach the checkered flag.

Sand Yachting

Acceleration

The acceleration provided by the wind is amazing on blowy days, and lying just a few inches from the ground on your back with your feet outstretched in front of you will guarantee you the ride of your life. The "Need For Speed" sand yachts can reach speeds of three times the wind speed, with a recent world record of 116 mph!

There are clubs all around the country, and courses available, so go on, give it a try!

The photographs on these pages were taken on a gusty winter day on a beach in Lincolnshire, UK.

Hang-gliding and Paragliding

World-class paraglider Mark Hayman talks about an extreme sport that is on the up and up.

Up, Up and Away!

"The thermals are really pulling through now. Time to go! A final check of the equipment and I'm ready for take-off. The wing kites up beautifully in the breeze, and in three paces I'm off the cliff face and flying. It's always a fantastic moment when you quit the ground and feel the power of the rising air tugging at you, like the wind calling a sailor to the sea.

Hang-gliding and paragliding are becoming very popular.

Mark Hayman flies above Lake Annecy.

Thermal Energy

I quickly hit the first really good mountainside thermal and turn hard into the core. Soon I'm rising at five, then ten, then fifteen feet per second. I'm away! The altitude that I gained from the thermal means that I can cross Lake Annecy and reach the mountain range on the other side."

Hang-gliding and Paragliding

A Truly Beautiful Perspective
Two paragliders float beautifully over a lake in France! Extreme sports are most widely practiced in some of the most beautiful areas of the world. This doubles the thrill as you experience top-action sport and breathtaking scenery at the same time.

Hang-gliding and Paragliding

Cloudbase

1. "Rocketing up the face of Mont Blanc, I'm quickly at cloudbase, and off on my route. Looking down at the peaks, I wave to all the climbers just below. How strange that it took them a whole day to get to the same place I just flew to in ten minutes!

Huge Thermals

Just over two hours later and I'm at 12,000 ft. in the middle of a huge mountainside thermal. The forces on my body are unreal, and the wing is dancing all over the sky. Boy, it's cold this high!

As the Eagle Flies

Rising into cloud I have to use the compass before bursting back into the sunlight high over Lake Annecy—an eagle flies past close enough to touch.

Superb Memories

The lake shimmers 10,000 ft. below, crossed by tiny sailing boats. I land after eight hours and 100 miles with a head full of superb memories. This is what I learned to fly for!"

A rigid-winged hang-glider flying high above Lake Annecy, France.

Skiing Off-Piste

Skiing through fresh powder snow is an amazing feeling. On the steep off-piste slopes it feels like floating down through soft pillows of snow.

Woody Bouma Showing the Way!

1. Improved ski technology, combined with skiers borrowing and enhancing snowboarding tricks, has allowed modern freestyle skiers to compete with snowboarders in the park and pipe.

Ski Waxing

2. Always remember to wax your skis prior to going out on the slopes. It will make your skis glide more efficiently, allowing you greater speed. It also helps to protect the equipment from the ravages of the climate and environment.

Skiing Off-Piste

Word of Warning

1. If you plan to ski off-piste, you must always be accompanied by an experienced guide. If you are lucky enough to be there on a good powder day, you will remember it forever.

Safety Equipment

2. As in all extreme sports, safety is important. When skiing off-piste, an "avalanche peep" is essential to ensure that if you get caught in one you can be rescued, or come to the aid of others.

Backpack

It's a good idea to have an avalanche probe, first-aid kit, a shovel, water, safety blanket, and nowadays a cellphone in your backpack! Many resorts now have cellphone access, so it's always a good idea to carry one, if not for emergencies, then to boast to your friends!

Downhill Skiing

Downhill skiing takes immense skill, fast reactions, co-ordination, and plenty of practice!

Downhill skiing is a very fast and dangerous sport. The skiers can reach speeds of around 90 mph heading down the mountains, taking corners at nearly the same velocity, and are often airborne, sometimes traveling 60 ft. or more before landing and continuing down the mountain.

Safety wear is minimal with a crash helmet being the only protection; the ski suit is designed purely for aerodynamics.

Downhill skiers reach speeds of 90 mph.

Kayaking

Shaun Baker is the world's premier extreme kayaker. Here he offers a brief insight into why he took up this sport.

In Trouble

"I used to drive my Mom mad. She said that as a kid, if there was ever water around, then I would be in it… usually in trouble.

First Canoe

My parents bought me my first canoe (or "kayak") in an attempt to control my dangerous behavior—I was ten years old and I was instantly addicted.

Experience

As the years passed, I progressed onto the violent white water of the big weirs on the River Thames, then by the age of fourteen onto expeditions—the longest being 700 miles of sea and white water, over $2^1/_2$ months when I was sixteen. Having survived these formative years, the allure of enormous waterfalls began to bite, and I was drawn to a waterfall in Wales that had never been run. It was nearly 50 ft. of pure freefall, and it gave me my first taste of spinal compression… and a new Guinness World Record. In Iceland in 1997, I pushed this record to nearly 65 ft., and in subsequent years I took three more records, including a kayak speed record… on snow!"

Rafting requires less training, but still gives you the thrill of white water.

Shaun Baker drops a 60 ft waterfall.

Kayaking

Shaun Baker kayaking down a water dam!

BMX

BMX was a massive sport during the 1980s. Today it is as popular as ever, and here, with Gary Connery's jump off Beachy Head in England, we have the most extreme example of it.

Ultimate Jump
1. Gary looked at the 450 ft. cliff and decided that he could ride off it on his BMX and throw out his parachute, combining two great sports to bring you the ultimate BMX jump! With everything prepared, we arrived at the cliff on a sunny summer's morning with very light winds. Gary looked over the edge and dropped a stone with a ribbon tied to it to see what effect the light wind would have on it.

Moment of Truth
2. Gary drew back 50 yards and began to pedal. With a huge bunny hop he was out and over the cliff and into freefall. This was the moment of truth: would the parachute open...?   It did!

BMX

Safe Landing
Gary flew out to sea, turned back, and landed at the water's edge to huge applause from the cliff above! His bike was trashed but with Gary safe, the stunt was pulled off in style and with no injury—always a massive result!"

REMEMBER—NEVER, EVER TRY THIS YOURSELF!

Mountain Biking

Rob Weaver took up mountain biking as a teenager. A self-confessed biking "addict," he is now famous for combining extreme freestyle tricks, jumps, and racing.

Life's Obsession

1. "I have been riding and racing mountain bikes for nearly half my life now. It was my brother who inspired me to begin riding, and slowly, my addiction grew and my life began to revolve around the sport—in all of its various forms!

Cross-Country

2. Cross-country was my starting point, and for a few years I happily raced, but the excitement began to

wear away, and my friends and I sought a bigger and more exciting rush. I started racing downhill, beginning at regional races, and slowly progressed to racing the entire national circuit, traveling the whole country.

Mountain Biking

Downhill Thrill

3. There really is nothing that can compare to riding downhill. The feeling you get when you pin a technical section or nail a massive jump, it seems to lift all your senses to another level. You can go faster and ride better than you ever have done, you are left with no worries other than when you will next get to ride your bike again. It is complete escapism with the biggest rush you could ever wish for."

Safety First

4. Mountain biking is a thrilling sport in all of its various forms. The potential for injury is obvious from the pictures on these pages—falling from a big air jump or colliding with another rider or tree can be very painful. As you can see from this picture, bikers wear a lot of safety clothing to minimize the risk of injury.

Essential Kit

A strong bike is essential for extreme mountain biking. Other items that you need include a helmet and padded clothing. Ask your mountain biking club for advice.

Mountain Biking

Extreme Jumping
"One of the best feelings has got to be jumping. As you lift into the air it's like a moment of pure tranquility, no noise—just complete silence for that short time until you return to Earth as smoothly as possible. The feeling is unbelievable; the fear and the adrenaline combine to make the ultimate rush. As long as you survive, it's got to be the ultimate!"

A mountain biker competing in full safety gear.

Big Rushes
"When I was launching the avalanche barrier out in France, the drop was huge, so the fall seemed to take forever, but it was one of the biggest rushes I've ever had."

Jumping is an important part of the sport.

Mountain Biking

REMEMBER—NEVER, EVER TRY THIS YOURSELF!

Bungee Jumping

Bungee jumping was invented by the people of the Pentecost Island in the South Pacific.

Modern-day Bungee Jumping

First witnessed in the Pentecost Island in the South Pacific, bungee jumping was originally devised as a means of testing the manhood of tribesmen. It was brought into the 20th century, with elastic as opposed to vines, by four members of a dangerous sports club, who plunged over the 250 ft. Clifton Suspension Bridge in Bristol, UK, in the 1970s.

Open to All

With no training required, bungee jumping is an accessible extreme sport. During the summer months, bungee jump cranes pop up all over the world. For a fee, you can experience the thrill of dropping 100 feet suspended by a piece of elastic and bouncing back up again.

REMEMBER— NEVER, EVER TRY THIS YOURSELF!

Age restrictions apply for those wishing to undertake an organized bungee jump.

Cliff Jumping

Strictly for professional stuntmen, you can't get more extreme than cliff jumping. Whatever you do—don't try this yourself!

Mark Munson
The spectacular cliffs in Cornwall, UK, set the scene for Mark Munson's 80 ft. leap from a cliff into the sea.

Blind Faith
When stuntmen perform cliff jumps, they are often unable to see where they will land.

Planning
Each jump needs to be planned down to the last detail, taking account of tides, wind, and the slant of the cliff.

REMEMBER— NEVER, EVER TRY THIS YOURSELF!

BASE Jumping

BASE stands for "Building, Antennae, Span, and Earth." Strictly for stuntmen, BASE jumping is the most extreme sport in the world.

What is it?
BASE jumping consists of jumping from a fixed-to-earth site (building, antennae, or span) with a parachute on the jumper's back. The chute is either thrown out from the jumper's hand or tied to the structure, and it then unfurls as the jumper falls through the air.

Deadly Pursuit
If the chute does not open, the jumper is in serious trouble and may well be seriously injured or even die. This makes BASE jumping the most dangerous of all extreme sports.

Eiffel Extravaganza
Gary Connery is the man (pictured right) jumping through the center of the Eiffel Tower in Paris. The weather that day was terrible, with 25 mph winds and rain and sleet being blown through the tower.

The Big Jump
Gary leapt out from the Eiffel Tower, and his chute snapped open. As he came below the legs of the tower he was blasted out of the side by the wind. He hit the road, just missing all the traffic, and broke his ribs. After a week in hospital, Gary was released, and returned home.

Pictures Are Worth A Thousand Words
The pictures of his amazing stunt were published worldwide the next day.

BASE jumping Bridge Day, New River, Gorge Bridge, West Virginia, America (left).

BASE Jumping

The wind blasted Gary Connery into the road, causing him to break several ribs.

BASE Jumping

Gorge Du Verdon

"While on a white-water rafting photoshoot in the Gorge du Verdon in France, I came across Ben, a French fireman who was going to BASE jump into the gorge. As Ben made his way around the edge of the rock, we held our breath as he leapt out and started his freefall. As his chute opened, we all breathed with relief again as Ben floated safely to the valley floor below."

BASE jumping the Gorge du Verdon.

Motorsports

Photographing extreme sports is difficult. Here, the author describes photographing motorsports, beginning with taking pictures of offshore powerboating while strapped to a helicopter.

Extreme Photography

"To capture the death-defying feats featured in this book is not easy. Indeed, taking this sort of photography could qualify as an extreme sport in its own right!

Power Boating

As the helicopter takes off with me hanging out of the side, my legs dangling in the fast air, I am aware of awesome power. Out over the sea now, we are chasing an offshore powerboat 30 feet below the helicopter and doing over 120 mph.

Ferocious Power

The twin Lamborghini V12 engines in the boat roar ferociously as the boat leaps out of the water and back again, the helicopter blades and wind rush all contributing to the spine-tingling experience."

An offshore powerboat in action.

Motorsports

Motor Rallies

Rally cars race over public roads, often in poor condition, and attempt to keep to a specified schedule. The first motor rally was held in 1907 and went from Beijing (Peking) to Paris. Although modern races are shorter, the high-powered cars make this a thrilling sport to compete in and watch.

Rally Racing with Colin McRae

1. "I have been in fast cars in my time, but as this one accelerates away on a loose surface, I realize I'm in for a treat. As Colin weaves his way through the forest course, keeping the camera steady is almost impossible. There is nothing like heading sideways towards a tree at great speed with one of the world's greatest rally drivers who, at the last second, smoothly negotiates the track and propels us further down it, past the tree. Frighteningly awesome!"

Motorsports

Le Mans 24 hr
"Celebrating its 70th anniversary in 2003, the Le Mans 24-hour race is one of the world's most extreme motorsport events. Officially known as the Grand Prix D'Endurance, cars race continuously for 24 hours and travel more than 3,000 miles at speeds of more than 125 mph.

Burn Rubber
2. As I run to the first corner, a car in the fading light brakes hard into the corner, turning the brake discs molten red as fire leaps from the exhaust. Suddenly it slingshots down the straight—for sheer noise, adrenaline, power, and excitement nothing beats extreme motorsports!

The Pits
3. I am in the pits as the mechanics work furiously to repair the car—every second counts!"

Final Word

Below are a few ideas to keep you fresh and up to date on the very latest in extreme sports.

Magazines
Check out your local bookstore, which may have imported or hard-to-get mags from around the world. They carry a wealth of information, and have breakdowns of new developments in the world of extreme sports.

Internet
This is an obvious choice! Just enter the name of the sport that interests you into the search engine, and you're away! Always search the internet under the supervision of an adult, and after asking permission first.

Multimedia
You can learn some great moves by watching videos and DVDs of any extreme sport. Play them in slow motion, or frame by frame, so you can study each move carefully. In addition, there are some great extreme sports programs on TV!